There's a Hole in My Sidewalk

The Romance of Self-Discovery

Portia Nelson

ATRIA PAPERBACK
New York London Toronto Sydney New Delhi

BEYOND WORDS
Portland, Oregon

ATRIA
PAPERBACK
A Division of Simon & Schuster, Inc.
1230 Avenue of the Americas
New York, NY 10020

BEYOND WORDS
1750 S.W. Skyline Blvd., Suite 20
Portland, Oregon 97221-2543
503-531-8700 / 503-531-8773 fax
www.beyondword.com

Copyright © 2012 by Portia Nelson
Originally published by Popular Library © 1977, ISBN 0-445-03199-9
Previously published by Stonebarn © 1988, ISBN 978-0-96211-590-5
and by Beyond Words Publishing © 1993, ISBN 978-0-94183-187-1

All rights reserved, including the right to reproduce this book or portions thereof in any form whatsoever without the prior written permission of Atria Books/Beyond Words Publishing, Inc., except where permitted by law.

Managing editor: Lindsay S. Brown
Design: Devon Smith

First Atria Books/Beyond Words paperback edition October 2018

ATRIA PAPERBACK and colophon are trademarks of Simon & Schuster, Inc.
BEYOND WORDS PUBLISHING and colophon are registered trademarks of Beyond Words Publishing. Beyond Words is an imprint of Simon & Schuster, Inc.

For more information about special discounts for bulk purchases, please contact Simon & Schuster Special Sales at 1-866-506-1949 or business@simonandschuster.com.

The Simon & Schuster Speakers Bureau can bring authors to your live event.
For more information or to book an event, contact the Simon & Schuster Speakers Bureau at 1-866-248-3049 or visit our website at www.simonspeakers.com.

Manufactured in the United States of America

10 9 8 7 6 5 4 3 2 1

The Library of Congress has cataloged the 1993 edition as follows:

Nelson, Portia.
There's a hole in my sidewalk: the romance of self-discovery / by Portia Nelson.
p. cm.
Originally published: Los Angeles; Popular Library, 1977.
1. Self-realization. 2. Self-perception. 3. Maturation (Psychology). 1. Title.
BF637.S4N45 1993
158'.1—DC20

93-18380

ISBN: 978-1-58270-685-6
ISBN: 978-1-4516-8635-7 (ebook)

The corporate mission of Beyond Words Publishing, Inc.: *Inspire to Integrity*

"I am part of all
that I have met."
—TENNYSON

To all of you,
whoever you are,
I humbly dedicate this book.

PERSONAL NOTE

I choose to call these thoughts "pieces"... pieces of me. These pieces have had a bit of trouble finding a comfortable concept that would knit them into one book... just as I have had difficulty molding a multi-faceted misfit into one person.

More than anything, they are evidence, to me, that here in the middle of my life I have finally gained a small pin-point of self-awareness... false images stripped away... "through a glass darkly, but, now... face to face." No hiding, anymore, behind innocence and ignorance.

It isn't necessarily easier now... but I have a self that I trust and feelings and the experience are mine... not what I should feel... not what I was taught to feel and not something someone else felt that I admired and imitated. Knowing one's own feelings and being able to trust them is the difference between existing and living. So, that's what I have here, I guess... living and loving experiences... pieces of my small universe that can, I hope, be recognized by yours.

EDITOR'S NOTE

I am pleased to present the 35th Anniversary Edition of *There's a Hole in My Sidewalk*. This extraordinary book was originally published in 1977, and since then it has become a well-loved classic. The humor, inspiration, insight, and comfort found within these pages have touched thousands of people. *There's a Hole in My Sidewalk* is not just another book that sits on the shelf; it is a trusted friend people turn to time and again. I am thrilled to be reissuing a book that has offered so many people hope and inspiration.

The opening poem, "Autobiography in Five Short Chapters," has been quoted in more than two hundred books. This simple, elegant poem depicts a universal journey that is at once deeply human and unwaveringly straightforward, and has helped guide many on their own path to self-discovery. If you are familiar with only this poem, I think you will be delighted to read the entire work.

Portia Nelson's writing is a clear, honest depiction of self-reflection, inner conflict, personal struggle, and, ultimately, resilience, personal growth, and hope, which has resonated deeply with those making transitions in their lives. *There's a Hole in My Sidewalk* has been especially significant to those recovering from addiction, as well as their loved ones, and has been used in many 12-step and recovery programs. As the publisher of this book, Beyond Words is honored to contribute to this tradition.

In the late 1990s, I had the pleasure of spending time with Portia Nelson in New York where she lived at the time. What a lovely woman she was! Portia led an accomplished life and left us with an impressive legacy that spans an acting career, which includes her role in the classic movie *The Sound of Music*, her body of work as a singer and composer, which includes five solo albums on major labels, and her work as writer, a result of which you now have in your hands. Although Portia is no longer with us, she is here in spirit, speaking to our hearts from the pages ahead.

I am proud to help continue Portia's legacy with this special edition. To celebrate this milestone we are releasing the book in hardcover for the first time, thus creating an enduring package to hold this timeless classic. I know that this book will continue to have great meaning in numerous lives for many more years to come. My hope is that one of those lives will be yours.

Cynthia Black
President and Editor in Chief
Beyond Words Publishing

CONTENTS

A story of
ME in You
and
You in Me
in
Five Short Chapters

PROLOGUE

My life has been a series
of wonderful experiences.
It's a pity I wasn't there
for most of them.

AUTOBIOGRAPHY IN FIVE SHORT CHAPTERS

Chapter One

I walk down the street.
There is a deep hole in the sidewalk.
I fall in.
I am lost.... I am helpless.
It isn't my fault.
It takes forever to find a way out.

Chapter Two

I walk down the same street.
There is a deep hole in the sidewalk.
I pretend I don't see it.
I fall in again.
I can't believe I am in this same place.
But, it isn't my fault.
It still takes a long time to get out.

Chapter Three

I walk down the same street.
There is a deep hole in the sidewalk.
I see it is there.
I still fall in... it's a habit... but,
my eyes are open.
I know where I am.
It is *my* fault.
I get out immediately.

Chapter Four

I walk down the same street.
There is a deep hole in the sidewalk.
I walk around it.

Chapter Five

I walk down another street.

CHAPTER ONE

I don't know what I want sometimes,
But I know
that I want to know
what I want.
I know that once I know what I want
I will be able to get it.
Of course, I may not want what I get
when I get it....
But, at least
I'll know I don't want that!
Then, I can move on to something else
I don't know if I want.
That's progress!

You say you love me for who I am....
But...
who you think I am
is not *who* I am.

Therefore,
it's hard for me to be who I am
when we're together...

because...
I think I have to be
who you think I am.

Of course,
I don't know exactly who it is
you think I am...
I just know it isn't who I am.

Who am I?
Well...
Who I am is something I recognize
when someone tells me
who I am *not*.
At least, I *think* that's *not* who I am.
Maybe who I am *not*
is who I *am*!
If that's who I am... MY GAWD...
you really love me.

I used to suffer a great deal
thinking I was the only one
in the world
so lonely
and troubled.

Then, I opened the door to myself
and discovered there were
millions
of people
just like me.

It isn't lonely anymore...
but it's miserable to be
so ordinary.

I know why we are friends.
It's because I don't always
approve of you.

You don't think you deserve approval.
So... if I gave it to you,
you would not
approve of me
and I would lose your trust.

Friendship is based on trust
and I want you
to trust me
because I need your approval.

However, if I get your approval,
I will not trust you
because I don't think I deserve approval
either.

I know why we are friends.

You want to please me… and,

I want to please you…

so please make the decision
about where we are going tonight.

If I make the decision…
and then *you* don't like it,
you'll be mad at me
and I'll be miserable all evening
because I haven't pleased you.

Now… if *you* try to please me…
and *you* make the decision,
and I don't like it
when we get there…
at least *you* will be pleased.

If I am unhappy with where we are,
or what we are doing,
that alright…

because it won't be my decision
that will have made you unhappy.
It will be yours.
Therefore,
it will be *your* fault!
That will please me.

You say you will never leave me
because I understand you.
And I love being thought of
as "understanding."

But, I also understand
that by being so understanding,
you automatically
have the freedom
to do as you please...
because...
if I am not understanding,
you will leave me.

I think that what I really
have to understand is this:
In order to be so understanding all the time
(so that you will not leave me),
I have to leave myself.

If I am not myself
when I am being so understanding,
who the hell is it
you will never leave?

Better I should not be so understanding
so there's somebody
you can leave.

You have made a fool of me!

I know that I am not the most beautiful,
the most talented, the most intelligent
person in the world...
but I liked you...
and I wanted you
to think I was.
So... I tried to be beautiful
talented and intelligent
for you.

However,
since I succeeded
in making you believe it,
naturally,
I immediately
lost respect for you
for not seeing
that I had fooled you.

Now...
I am intelligent enough,
beautiful enough and
talented enough

not to be associated with fools…
and I am incensed that I didn't see
how foolish you were
at once.

But…
I liked you then… and…
it drove me to make you believe
what I wanted you to believe….

Except…
I was so convincing,
I began to believe it myself!

Now…
anybody who believes
things like that about me
is a fool.

That makes me a fool!

And if it weren't for you
believing what I wanted you to believe,
I wouldn't know that.

I hate you for making a fool of me!

Will you please stop trying to
finish my sentences before I do?

It's humiliating!

After all... it's my sentence!
Let me show it off!

I know you are really trying to let me know
how sensitive and smart you are...
and how deeply you understand me....

But... if you are that smart...
please let me think that
I am smarter than you
by not impressing me with
how smart you are
in the middle of my sentences!

Of course,
if I am smart enough
to be aware of
what you are up to…

Then,
I should be smart enough to know
it doesn't matter what you do
in the middle of my sentences.

Maybe I'm not so smart!

Now, that *is* humiliating!

I want you to love me…
but I am aware
that you only love
what you cannot get.
So, I can't let you know
that I am interested
or you won't love me back.

Now…
I hate games
and dishonesty
more than anything.

Therefore…
if I love you enough
to be dishonest…
to play a game
in order to keep you interested,
I will hate myself.
If I hate myself,
eventually,
I will crack up!

If I crack up…
at least,
you won't be able to get me…
because I won't care…
or be aware
that you even exist…
and then,
maybe you will love me.

Jesus! There's got to be a simpler way!

You are strong... vital...
very much in control of yourself.
I admire that!
I know you can help me...
and I need help.

But,

if I allow you to help me,
I will have to trust you enough
to give up my own self control.

If I give that up,
I will begin to feel powerless...
without identity...
like a nobody!

How dare you help me to be a nobody!

I cannot seem to leave you…
though often,
I think I should because
even though I care…
I am not in love with you.
But I am in love with the fact
that you are in love with me.
It makes me think very well of myself,
When I think well of myself,
I am very nice…
and very creative.
That makes me feel worthwhile and then
I love myself.
The more I love myself…
the more you love me.
No wonder I can't leave.
I wouldn't know
I loved myself…
without you.

I would like to be one…
A one not worried about being two!
I am more one
when we are three.
When we are two,
I become a zero.
I become zero because
I am afraid you will see
that I am not one.
When we are three, I am comfortable…
It doesn't matter if I am not one
since I seem to become one
simply because
there are two being two
and letting me be one.
Therefore, I am not zero… I can't be…
Two from there is always one.
So, I am more one when we are three…
as long as I don't worry about
being two.

In the beginning
everywhere I went,
I didn't always go along.
I didn't know it then,
but I was afraid I'd meet myself
When we finally met,
I wasn't who I expected I'd be…
but, oh, it was a relief
to have someone to be with…
at last.

CHAPTER TWO

I am a hopeless romantic
who does not believe
love solves everything.
Still, I weep for the loss
of illusion…
knowing full well
that reality
is unbearable…
without a few gilded window frames
to see through.

How brazen you are!

You lean across the table…
slender hands
cupping your face…

and stare arrow-straight
into my eyes…
no blinking at all.

You know you are making a frame

for a remarkably beautiful face.

I stare back…
not out of desire
or challenge…

but as my only defense
against your discovering

how deeply I am immersed in pleasure.

I hope that what you are after
is an exchange…
not
a reaction.

One step forward
into the bright of loving.
Yet, I fear the bright will not last.
... so, one step back.
Still, I fear more,
the dark of not loving at all.
Well then...
may I take a giant step?
May I?
I have already answered.
Shall we dance?

I know who you are.

You are so much of me
that if I don't love you
I won't exist.

And I'm selfish.
I don't want to miss anything.

Two days ago
I never would have believed
I would spring from my bed
at the first glimmer
of sunlight…
and drive all over town
looking for
blue Volkswagens!

Dear one…

Kind one…

lend me your dreams
for a while.

Cover me
with the sweet sleep
of your innocence,
and wake me
with the crystal sunshine
of your hope.

Light my darkness with fireflies
and build me air castles
to house
the velvet summers
of love.

Stay with me,
dear one…
stay with me long enough
to let me hear again,
that far away music
of yesterday…
when I was young.

Your hair is like a monk's cap
made of wheat.

It often slips down over your eyes
so I can't see if you are
hiding from me
or spying on me.

Sometimes
I reach out...
as an artist might...
and make a gentle brush stroke
on the canvas of your brow
to change the shape of your cap.

As much as I love it,
I cannot bear to talk to you
without watching your eyes.

Besides,
there is such selfish pleasure
in the act of touching,
lightly...
hardly at all...
making a graceful arc there
and seeing you smile...
as if your hair were attached
to the corners of your mouth.

There is so much about me that I don't know until I talk to you.

That first day...
as you turned to leave...
we touched...
and, like magnets, we clung to one another
for a long time.
Nothing more.
Yet...in that rare moment of holding you
I experienced what I have come to value most...
the ecstasy
of
not doing anything
about it.

How wise of you to wait…
to fill the shy, awkward spaces
with white wine
and cushioned conversation.
I am aware that you are
allowing me time
to become accustomed
to the cities of your smile…
and to window shop your eyes…
until, at last,
I am so full of you,
that I no longer blush
on my way into your arms.

Water, Air, Earth, Fire.

Mix together slowly,
with ceiling seagulls
and pear wine.

Stir until the perfect blend…

Cool for a moment… then,
place in the fruitful womb
of love
to be born again
into a circle of light…

an enchanted world where only believers
are allowed to enter.

I can feel my fear beginning
to settle inside me...
like sleepy kittens
upon the hearth
Shshshsh... tip toe...
Don't slam doors in my mind...
not now.
Let the kittens sleep a little while
please...
The fire will die soon enough, anyway...
And now, while the world is warm...
hold me.

I think I just fell into a hole
in the sidewalk.

I have said, "I love you"...
before you,
and meant it.

Yet,
I would have to admit...
that laid on the scales,
the pain of loving
has often outweighed the joy.

But, it never ceases to amaze me
that I never died of love.

Looking back...
knowing I survived...
pain has become my faith.

Though I am fragile...
it is my strength.

So, I warn you...
I will not die of you.

I know that pain and joy
cannot be separated…
and, like tomorrow and today
they become one another.

And so, I remember those
before you,
and rejoice that I said,
"I love you"
before you…

because,
it will help me not to die of you…
like I didn't
before you.

I am always a grumbling sleepwalker
in the mornings.

Do you realize...
for three days in a row
I have laughed
at least ten times
before coffee?

It's a dreary day....
Let's just stay inside.
We can pretend that
Kisses are brushes
and that we are
each other's canvases.
We won't need a northern light...
or any light at all,
for that matter....
And who cares if we ever finish
the picture, anyway.

Sorry I didn't answer.
I was listening
to what you weren't saying.

You are the oldest young person
I have ever known.
It makes me feel younger than you are.
That's a neat trick!

I am so free with you,
I never wish to be
free of you.

The beautiful togetherness
of our silence
makes me wonder
why we ever bothered
to speak at all.

I didn't really
leave my heart
in San Francisco…
although I said I did….
But, I certainly
let it out
into the fresh
morning air
and ran it up and down
a few hills.
I did let it rest
in the smile
of a beautiful stranger
for a few days…
But then,
I snatched it away
and brought it home
to you…
as I knew I would
before I went away
to be mad at you.

I think I love you most
in those early hours
just before sunrise
When,
spent with loving
and lost in dreaming,
You reach out,
like the morning glory vine,
and wind about,
braiding limb to limb,
binding me to you
with the tender quiet
of us.
Desire is buried in slumber…
and,
asking nothing…
giving all…
You bend to touch me
through a thousand years of knowing
…without knowing.
But I know.
I'm glad I'm a light sleeper.

When I listen
to your feelings,
and can feel
your listenings...
Only then
can I expect you
to hear me.

We are not "in love"…
but, we are love.
I'm glad.
It lasts longer.

My longing is burning a hole
in my patience....
Time is spinning away.
What good is sleep
when an eternity
is rushing by
that I could be kissing you?

Damn it!
Will you please wake up?
I think I'll turn over...
a little bump
never hurt anybody!
"Hey!...awake so early?
I love you."

Please understand…
There are days I must leave you…
in order to be closer to you.
Up close, I cannot search out
those fragments of you
that your image of yourself
hides from me.
At a distance…
uncluttered be sensation…
I can really see you, freely…
and discover pieces of myself,
as well.
And then, we come home together…
to love you all the more.

You said you didn't love me
this morning.
I didn't believe you.
I knew you just hated yourself.
That's alright.
I don't love you either…
today.

Please…
don't extract promises from me
that must race quickly
from the present
into the past
casting dark shadows on the future.
Now… today… is all
we can be certain of
and love
is something better
than a collection of pretty vows
to cling to on a rainy day.
What we already are
is what we will be
together.
Isn't that enough?

Stop looking at me like that!
Can't you see how much
I need you to believe
what I am saying
so that I can believe it
myself?

I would give you everything...
if I could... but,
the only gift worth giving
is freedom...
the freedom to grow...
away from me
if necessary.
Of course, one can't give freedom,
but, at least I know that.
Maybe that's the gift then...
the knowing....
And I couldn't tie a ribbon around it
even if I wanted to.

Ask something of me…
please.
I know there is no answer…
but often,
I need to feel it would be me
you would ask…
if there was one.

I am not locking out!
I am trying very hard
not to lock you in!
Maybe it's, the same thing

What you seek is my approval…
not my self.
So, it is more friendly
that I turn you
back to your self…
the source
of acceptance.
When you no longer need
my approval…
I can give it to you.

You say you love me
because I understand you
better than you understand
yourself.

Sometimes, like now,
I wish I didn't
because it forces me to see
that it is also the reason
you will have to
leave me.

You slept on your own side of the bed
last night....
It was a universe wide.
When I reached out to touch you
all I could feel
was the distance
between.
It is still there today.
Your eyes... that soft bed blue...
once my resting place...
are crowded with distant mountains
and racing rivers.
And I'll be alone...
with you...
again tonight.

This is no carnival!
I can ride with you…
but,
I am not
your
merry-go-round.
When you have discovered
the difference…
I'll meet you at the Ferris wheel.

I don't smoke…

so…

I never thought
I would miss the stale smell
of your bent,
charred cigarretes
on my bedside table.

But,

the clean ashtray
was as glaring
as a headlight,
last night.

I couldn't sleep.

If I smoked…

maybe I wouldn't have noticed
you were gone.

Maybe.

Let me be angry…
please.
It is the only way
I can keep you from seeing
how much
I need you.

If I say "no" to you
I will lose you.
If I say "yes"...
I will lose myself.
Even if I win, I lose.
Or do I?

I am not a piece of jewelry
to be worn
so that others will admire you.
If you choose to continue...
you must also remember
that when jewelry is displayed
...it can be stolen.

Will you try…just once,
to be my age?
I'm tired of
trying to be yours.

Stand up.
Let go of my hand.
Maybe then…
I can let go of yours.
You first.

I know you heard me…
but were you listening?

Better stop now,
before smiles become tightropes
for words that step…
with measured coolness…
across mechanical lips into deaf ear.

Please get the hell out of my life…
only…
go softly…
and don't let me see you go…
or I may call you back…
and there is no one home.

Wait!
You can't leave me now.
What will I do with all these
Oreo cookies?

I warn you…I will not die of you.

I warn you…I will not die of you.

The silence is so loud,
I cannot hear my own advice.

Love, love... where are you?
You alone soothe the ache...
and I cannot believe in you.

Today...
I know how lonely I am
for you.
I have mistakenly called
four people
by your name.

The most I can hope for,
right now,
is to make it to tomorrow…
just once…
without listening
for the phone.

I made the bed today.
I almost thought I was over you
... for a minute.

I never lied to you.
I always told you the truth
about love.

The joke is:
You listened to me.
I didn't.

CHAPTER THREE

I crowed
What I knowed
Bestowed
What I knowed
You hoed
What I knowed
And growed
What I knowed
But I slowed
What I knowed
And stowed
What I knowed
Then you goed
Up the road
And I blowed
What I knowed.

I know myself…
Now that you have left…
I shall be everywhere
hoping to make such memories
with someone else.
That is when I will really feel
you have gone.

My body is suspended…
My mind is lost in space…
My tongue just wobbles loosely
back and forth…
Saying nothing…
Doing nothing…
Out of time and out of place.
Like a bird… in dead of winter…
flying north.

What were you...?
Who were you...?
Something in me... I know that.
But you were like a drug.
While you were near,
you were the ultimate "high."
With you... I could split atoms,
stop time...
stay young...
Or I thought I could.
But you only gave out small doses of yourself,
enough to keep me coming back.
And I could never be sure
when you would be available again.
Soooo... the inevitable crash... withdrawal!
I won't break windows, kill,
or steal for a "fix"...
but I sometimes feel I might die
for need of you.

As with tennis…
never play "Love"
with someone
whose game
is not as good as yours.
You'll end up losing…
and they won't
know enough
to care.

Without ever having you…
I have lost you.
Without ever knowing you…
I know you…
There is no history…
Only a memory
that never occurred at all.
A memory…
I can never forget.

It was a certain kind of sun, then…
And dreams and hopes hung like thick smoke
in the air.
Lyrics of songs jumped out at me
like playful kittens around
a corner.
It is a long-remembered, half-forgotten time.
Where is it now?
Waiting for me…or for you…somewhere?
Or has it gone its way…
like the morning of your smile?

We weren't living together,
anyway.
We were hiding together.

"Pain and loneliness make you strong…"
I dish that one out a lot!
Today, I don't want to be strong.
I want to dream just as much
as anybody else.
But, I keep on paying my dues, anyway,
and I really don't want
to belong
to that club
anymore.

You were so busy finding yourself
in me…
That I had to run from you
To keep you from killing
both of us.

Have you learned yet,
That who you know
is not
who you are?

The softer I walk
The louder I hear.

To own anything
is to be owned by it.
I never wanted to own you....
It's impossible....
And I never wanted to be owned.
But, I guess
I always wanted you
to pretend
that you thought
I was worth owning.

If all the "ifs" and "maybes,"
"wish-I-weres" and
"could-have-beens-
if-only-things-
were-different-
than-they-are"
could fall right off a cliff...
maybe I'd discover how
to live with
what is here and now...
but then,
I might as well forget this
'cause I started it
with "if."

In those moments of despair…
when I really don't care
whether or not I survive,
then, am I most keenly aware
of the certainty that I will.
That's the pain of it…
and the miracle.

CHAPTER FOUR

I am astounded
at how long it takes
to discover…
for the first time,
the things I have learned…
over and over again
all my life.

The real growth
is in recognizing
that we do
always get
what we want in life…
one way or another.

Nobody's perfect!
Somebody doesn't have to be.

Most loneliness
is pain...
peering into mirrors
of self-pity
with the hope
of seeing someone else
to blame it on.

Listen to what you criticize
most severely
And you will hear
what you most fear
you are.

I was always afraid of
risking *risk*.
But I found that I could stand
to risk *risk*
better than I could stand
to fear *fear*.
At least, risking
brought about changes…
and the changes took up so much time,
I forgot what it was I was afraid
to risk losing…
in the first place.

The nicest thing about my life, now, is
that I am here with me
most of the time.

There is no such thing
as perfect freedom…
There is only the freedom to
discover
that there is
no such thing
as perfect freedom!

It is much easier to be lonely
without someone…
than it is to be lonely
with someone.

Real belief
is a quiet thing...
too busy being itself
to look for disciples.

It is a waste of time and energy
to worry about
what others are thinking
about you.

because...

You can never know
exactly what another person
is thinking...AND,
the worst part it...
they are usually not thinking
about you at all.

They are too busy worrying about
what others
are thinking about them.

So, the truth is, all those terrible thoughts
you thought they might
be thinking about you,
are your own thoughts
about yourself.

Better spend your energy
worrying about that…or,
you just might
convince somebody to think
what you were afraid
they might be thinking
after all.

It isn't always best
to let everything
spill out.
At times,
there is more to be gained
by using restraint!
Remember,
it is the water
held back by the dam
that lights the city!

Always trying
to be a good person
can be the biggest block
to becoming one.

To live happily with a pet,
one must first accept
the responsibility
of disciplining it
consistently and firmly
with much love!
To live happily with ourselves...
it is the same.

Who you are
is not
who you were…
It is who you are.

Any day of the week
I would choose to be "out"
with others
and in touch
with myself...
than to be "in" with others
and out of touch
with myself.

I can tell how secure I am now.
I no longer clean the house
the day before the maid comes!

Love is not a thing
to be "in" or "out" of.
It just is.
The beginning is the ending...
and the ending... the beginning...
Always and
never...
forever.

In youth...
man seems to satisfy loneliness
with passion....
And in maturity...
aloneness... with compassion.
What a pity the difference
is most often discovered
after muscle and bone
can no longer climb
to the top
of the mountain.

I have come to regard unrequited love
like a hole in a sock.
Mend it, or discard it!
Don't just stand there with cold feet!

Disciplining one's self
can be carried
too far.
It is alright to relax
part of the time.
Even the soils is richer
when it rests
every seven years.

If I keep talking about
what I believe in...
Eventually...
I will tell myself
how much I believe in
what I talk about.

Since I've finally
taken responsibility
for my life—
I can't tell you how often
I've wanted
to give it back.

But, nobody wants it.

Isn't that lucky?

Nothing matters, now.
I mean…
everything matters so much
that nothing matters now.

Alone can be beautiful.
It's the one truth
we know to be certain.
We are
A Lone.
To embrace that truth
is the first step
to becoming
Al One!

CHAPTER FIVE

I walk down another street.

Aware and alive
to the little I know,
as if I've arrived
at another plateau.
A plateau... familiar...
yet,
wonderfully strange
where I find my milieu
in the fortunes of change.

In my soul is a room
with a wedding inside....
Alone
is the groom
and Truth is
the bride.

Pity has gone
to its place on a shelf…
to be summoned for others
but
rarely for self.
Touching and feeling
in heart and in brain
Accepting the healing
of joy
that's in pain….

Where *Alone* is not gloom,
nor a fearsome divide.
Alone is the groom
and the Truth is
the bride.

Your alone-ness
nourishes and protects
my own.
I am always on the watch
for you.
No need to wear a carnation!
I'll know you…by me…
but you can hurry
if you want to.

EPILOGUE

I know you, by me…
and me, by you.
A mirrored exchange
of awareness…loving.
Loving awareness…
Always becoming…
becoming always
more you in me
and me in you…
Growing separately together…
changing and remaining the same,
eternally.

ABOUT THE AUTHOR

Portia Nelson was a renaissance woman: author, singer, actress, composer, lyricist, painter, and photographer. She has appeared in such films as *The Sound of Music*, *Dr. Dolittle*, *The Trouble with Angels*, and *The Other*, as well as on the television soap opera *All My Children*, as Mrs. Gurney for many years. She performed on Broadway in the award-winning musical *The Golden Apple*.

Over the years she has written the music and lyrics for many revues, television specials, and films. Her song "Make a Rainbow" was sung by Marilyn Horne at President Clinton's inaugural ceremony.

As a singer, Ms. Nelson recorded five show albums for Columbia Records and three additional solo albums. She was also included in the Smithsonian collections *Cole Porter Songs* and *The American Popular Song*.

There's a Hole in My Sidewalk was made into a musical based on the book, and played at the York Theatre in Manhattan. Portia directed, wrote both the music and lyrics, and performed in the production.

There's a Hole in My Sidewalk was originally published in 1977 by Popular Library and was reprinted by the author in 1988. Since that time, the book has become a sought-after classic, but very hard to find. The poem "Autobiography in Five Short Chapters" has been reprinted in numerous publications. If you wish to use any of the material in this book, please contact the publisher.